DISCOVER&
LEARN

KW-136-091

RAINFORESTS

by
Joanna Brundle

Photo Credits

Images are courtesy of Shutterstock.com. With thanks to Getty Images, Thinkstock Photo and iStockphoto.

Cover – Chansom Pantip, 4&5 – Sorn340 Images, eAlisa, bogadeva1983, reisegraf.ch, Banach Ewelina, 6&7 – Kirasolly, Nowaczyk, Ondrej Prosicky, feathercollector, 8&9 – KayaMe, Ondrej Prosicky, Alessandro Pierpaoli, pisces2386, Tonio_75, 10&11 – Dr Morley Read, Shulevskyy Volodymyr, Ondrej Prosicky, Pedro Helder Pinheiro, 12&13 – SL-Photography, Ryan M. Bolton, Paman Aheri, Juhku, 14&15 – Kagai19927, Usanee, Jeff Holcombe, Josanel Sugasti, Ryan M. Bolton, 16&17 – Anna Veselova, dvigalet, Cristian Gusa, Dennis van de Water, Kevin Wells Photography, 18&19 – Ghing, Warawich Suyasa, Babu Paul, Erik Zandboer, 20&21 –Yatra, BestForBest, Heike Rau, 22&23 – Gustavo Frazao, fivespots, Hand Denis Schneider, Toniflap, buteo, 24&25 – Thammanoon Khamchalee, Rich Carey, Alex East, Roman Rybaleov, 26&27 – FloridaStock, Alexandros Michailidis, Jeroen Mikkers, 28&29 – K I Photography, dolphfyn, Dennis Wegewijs, Rob Crandall, 30&31 – gary yim, massdon, sma1050.

![BookLife Publishing logo]

BookLife
PUBLISHING

©2020
BookLife Publishing Ltd.
King's Lynn
Norfolk PE30 4LS

ISBN: 978-1-83927-079-6

Written by:
Joanna Brundle

Edited by:
William Anthony

Designed by:
Gareth Liddington

All rights reserved.
Printed in Malaysia.

A catalogue record for this book
is available from the British Library.

All facts, statistics, web addresses and URLs in this book were verified as valid
and accurate at time of writing. No responsibility for any changes to external
websites or references can be accepted by either the author or publisher.

CONTENTS

Words that look like **this** are explained in the glossary on page 31.

WHAT ARE
RAINFORESTS?

Tropical rainforests are hot, **humid** forests that grow near the Equator, in an area known as the tropics. They cover only a tiny amount of the Earth, but they are home to over half the Earth's animal and plant **species**.

Mammals such as sloths and monkeys, **reptiles** such as snakes and chameleons, birds such as eagles and parrots, and insects such as ants and butterflies all live in rainforests. Thousands of species of trees, flowering plants, shrubs and ferns provide food for plant eaters that, in turn, provide food for meat eaters.

COLOURFUL RAINFOREST ORCHIDS

HOWLER MONKEY

Rainforests have been around for millions of years, since the time of the dinosaurs. Tropical rainforests receive strong sunlight and very heavy rainfall of over 2,000 millimetres a year. Temperatures are very warm throughout the year, rarely falling below 20 degrees Celsius, even at night.

The world's largest tropical rainforests are the Amazon rainforest in South America and the Congolese rainforest in Africa. Australia has a small rainforest in Queensland, and in Asia the largest rainforest stretches across Indonesia.

RAINFORESTS PROVIDE A RANGE OF habitats FROM THE FOREST FLOOR UP TO THE HIGHEST BRANCHES.

ASIA

THE TROPICS

THE EQUATOR

Amazon rainforest

AFRICA

Congolese rainforest

SOUTH AMERICA

AUSTRALIA

Temperate rainforests lie outside the tropics. They have high rainfall but colder weather than tropical rainforests.

LET'S TAKE A
CLOSER LOOK

Rainforests are made up of different layers. Each has its own plant and animal species which are **adapted** to the different amounts of sunlight and rainfall reaching each layer.

EMERGENT LAYER

CANOPY LAYER

UNDERSTOREY LAYER

FOREST FLOOR

KAPOK TREES ARE FOUND IN THE EMERGENT LAYER.

Unlike animals, plants are able to make their own food, which they need in order to live and grow. They make food using water, **carbon dioxide** from the air, and sunlight. In the rainforest, plants compete for sunlight. Only the strongest trees reach the highest level, known as the emergent layer. This layer receives bright sunshine all year round and is also very hot and windy.

EMERGENT LAYER

The tallest trees in the emergent layer can grow over 70 metres (m) tall. They have wide, spreading tops and tough, waxy leaves that give protection from the sunlight. The strong winds and height from the forest floor help to scatter the seeds of these trees. They also make the emergent layer a dangerous place to live.

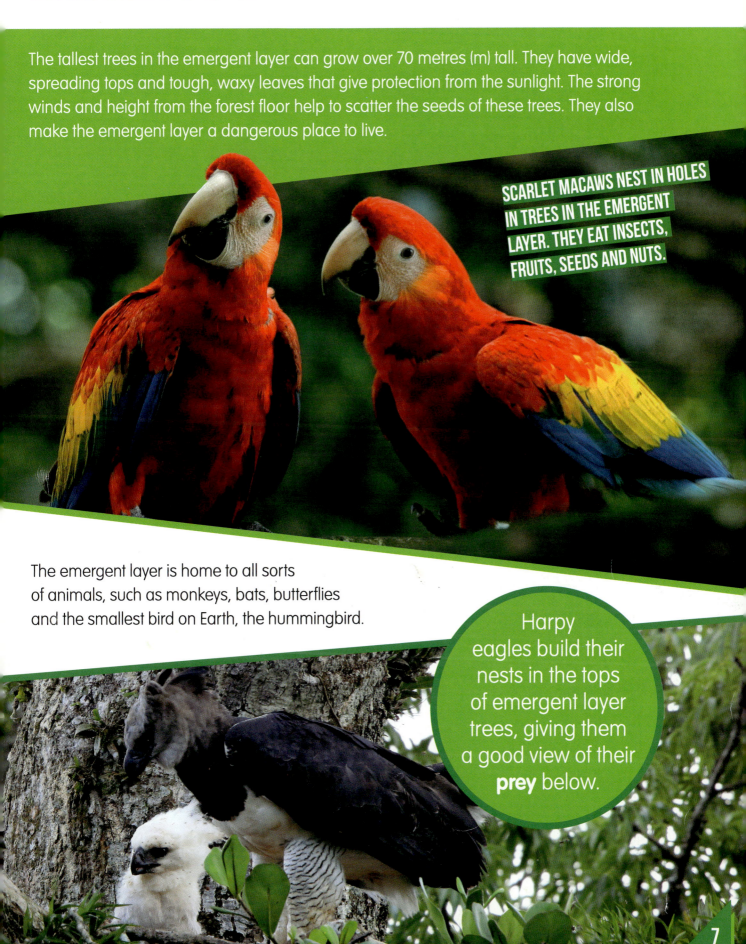

SCARLET MACAWS NEST IN HOLES IN TREES IN THE EMERGENT LAYER. THEY EAT INSECTS, FRUITS, SEEDS AND NUTS.

The emergent layer is home to all sorts of animals, such as monkeys, bats, butterflies and the smallest bird on Earth, the hummingbird.

Harpy eagles build their nests in the tops of emergent layer trees, giving them a good view of their **prey** below.

THE CANOPY

THE THICK CANOPY LAYER STOPS MOST OF THE SUNLIGHT FROM REACHING THE UNDERSTOREY LAYER.

The canopy is made up of trees that reach a height of about 40 m. Their leaves and branches spread out to form a thick canopy, like a giant umbrella, that shades the layers underneath.

Many animals, such as this squirrel monkey, take shelter in the canopy from forest floor **predators**. Some never come down to the forest floor.

Thanks to the plentiful rain and sunlight reaching the canopy, there is lots of food for the many species that live here, including squirrel monkeys, tree frogs, bats and snakes. From the air, the canopy looks like a continuous layer. However, most trees do not touch one another and animals have to fly, glide or leap between them.

SQUIRREL MONKEY

Thick, climbing vines called lianas are common in the canopy. They begin life on the ground, but then attach themselves to trees and climb upwards in search of sunlight. Lianas often become tangled together, forming networks and pathways that animals use to help them move about.

LIANAS LOOK LIKE ROPES HANGING IN THE RAINFOREST. THEY CAN GROW TO HUNDREDS OF METRES IN LENGTH.

Some beautiful flowering plants, such as orchids and bromeliads, are not attached to the ground. They grow on other plants instead, and they are common in the canopy. Some plants, such as the strangler fig, eventually smother and kill the tree that supports them.

The thick, waxy leaves of a bromeliad form a bowl shape that catches water and gives a home to frogs, snails and beetles.

STRANGLER FIG

THE UNDERSTOREY

The hot, humid understorey is quite dark because it only gets a small amount of sunlight. The plants that grow here often have large, dark-green leaves to catch as much sunlight as possible. They include small trees, low-lying shrubs, ferns, climbing plants and bananas.

Mosses, **fungi** and **algae** grow on tree trunks and branches. If a canopy tree dies and falls over, understorey trees can grow very quickly to fill in the gap. The few flowering plants are often brightly coloured or strong smelling to attract bees and butterflies.

BRIGHTLY COLOURED HELICONIA

The understorey has perfect conditions for the insects that live there, including bees, stick insects, moths and butterflies. These insects are food for birds, bats, monkeys, frogs and lizards.

GLASSWING BUTTERFLY

THERE IS VERY LITTLE WIND IN THE UNDERSTOREY TO SCATTER THE SEEDS OF PLANTS. SEEDS ARE SPREAD ON THE BODIES AND IN THE DUNG (POO) OF ANIMALS.

The pattern of a jaguar's coat helps it to blend into its surroundings until it is ready to pounce.

The understorey's humidity also makes it an ideal habitat for creatures such as tree frogs and salamanders that need to stop their moist skin from drying out. Understorey trees are home to large predators such as jaguars. They wait on the lookout in the branches and hunt at night.

THE FOREST FLOOR

FUNGI

The forest floor is very shady as little sunlight
reaches this layer. It is, however, a very important part of the rainforest,
because this is where decomposition (rotting) takes place. The dark, moist floor means dead plants
and animals that have fallen down will rot quickly. Fungi and **microorganisms** recycle and feed on
nutrients from the rotting material, beginning the **food chain**. Termites, spiders, cockroaches and
centipedes also live on the forest floor.

Scorpions feed on insects and spiders.

The forest floor is where some of the rainforest's largest animals are found. Depending on where the rainforest is, these animals might include tigers, pumas, ocelots, tapirs, armadillos and warthogs.

Tigers live in the tropical rainforests of South Asia.

BUTTRESS TREE ROOTS

Rainforest soil is poor, with nutrients only found near the surface, so tree roots are usually shallow. This can make trees unstable, so some produce buttress roots. These roots grow out from the trunk, as much as 4.5 m above the ground, and support the tree. They also spread out around the bottom of the tree, helping it to reach soil nutrients from farther away.

ADAPTING TO RAINFOREST LIFE

All living things have to adapt to their environment in order to survive. Every habitat is home to plants and animals that are specially adapted to live there. The leaves of canopy plants have pointed ends, called drip tips, that help rainwater to run off them easily. Without this adaptation, the leaves would quickly rot.

DRIP TIP

PITCHER PLANTS

The smell of the pitcher plants' nectar attracts insects. The insects fall into the nectar and become the pitcher plants' food. Inside each pitcher are small hairs that point downwards to stop the insects escaping.

Sloths are very well **camouflaged** and move extremely slowly, making them very difficult for predators to spot. They spend so much of their time asleep or perfectly still that algae can grow on their fur. The green colour of the algae provides extra camouflage. Sloths can turn their heads almost all the way round, helping them to spot predators.

Sloths use their strong claws to cling on to tree branches.

The flying frog is adapted to move easily around the canopy. It has webbed hands and feet and a flap of loose skin that stretches between its limbs when it jumps, so it can glide between branches.

The toucan is a colourful canopy bird. Its long bill helps it to reach fruit on branches that would be too weak for it to stand on and that other birds cannot reach. The bill also has a saw-like edge that helps the toucan to grasp its food and to peel fruit. It can also use its bill to control its body temperature, so that it does not overheat.

THE TOUCAN'S COLOURS PROVIDE CAMOUFLAGE IN THE LIGHT OF THE CANOPY.

Aye-ayes tap on trees using their long middle fingers. They then listen for bugs moving under the bark and use their long middle fingers to scoop them out.

AYE-AYES ALSO USE THEIR LONG FINGERS TO EAT COCONUTS AND FRUITS.

The blue morpho butterfly has many adaptations that help it to survive. A flash of its bright blue wings startles predators. The large eyespots on the underside of its wings may trick predators into thinking it is a much larger animal.

EYESPOTS

Leafcutter ants are adapted to carry things many times heavier than themselves. They bite leaves into pieces that they carry back to their nests underground. They then feed on fungus that grows on the leaves.

AFTER DARK

Nocturnal animals are those that are mainly active during the night. They sleep during the day and hunt or feed after dark. At night, rainforests are teeming with nocturnal creatures, including moths, owls, armadillos and some types of snakes and beetles.

WINGSPAN

THE ATLAS MOTH IS ONE OF THE BIGGEST INSECTS ON EARTH WITH A WINGSPAN OF UP TO 30 CENTIMETRES (CM).

Some nocturnal creatures, such as tarsiers, have huge eyes that help them to see in dim light. Each of the tarsier's eyes can weigh as much as its brain. Tarsiers also have excellent hearing. They move their large ears constantly to help them find their prey in the dark.

The emerald tree boa is a nocturnal predator that lives in the canopy. By day, it loops itself around tree branches, but at night it creeps up on its prey, pounces and then squeezes its victim to death.

Emerald tree boas are carnivores (meat eaters) that eat lizards, frogs, squirrels and small monkeys.

THE EMERALD TREE BOA CAN LAST WEEKS WITHOUT A MEAL.

Flying foxes are found in rainforests in Madagascar, Australia and Asia.

Flying foxes, also known as fox bats, have wide, leathery wings and fox-like faces. They live in huge groups called colonies, hanging upside down in trees by day. At night, they use their excellent sight and sense of smell to find the fruits, nectar and flowers that they like to eat.

RAINFOREST
RESOURCES

Resources are valuable or useful items. Many natural resources, such as rubber, are found in rainforests.

Rubber is made from a milky, white liquid called latex, taken from rubber trees.

COCOA PODS CONTAIN SEEDS THAT ARE USED TO MAKE COCOA BUTTER, WHICH IS FOUND IN cosmetics, CANDLES AND CHOCOLATE.

FOODS

Foods found in rainforests include fruits such as bananas, acai berries and pineapples. There are also spices such as vanilla, black pepper and cinnamon, and nuts including cashews and Brazil nuts. Coffee plants also grow in rainforests, along with cocoa trees.

WOOD

Rainforests contain many valuable hardwood trees, such as teak and mahogany. Wood from these trees is used to make furniture and flooring.

MEDICINE

Rainforest plants are used as ingredients in some of the most important medicines. This includes medicines for heart disease, malaria, fever and pain. Rainforest plants are also used to make antiseptics, which are used to clean wounds.

Quinine, a medicine used to treat malaria, is found in cinchona tree bark, which grows in Africa and South America.

Many antibiotics, used to treat infection, are made using rainforest plants. Some antibiotics are becoming less effective because they have been used too much. Fortunately, scientists think that, thanks to the huge range of plants in the rainforests, more antibiotics will be discovered.

THE AMAZON
RAINFOREST

A SQUARE KILOMETRE IS AN AREA THAT MEASURES ONE KILOMETRE IN WIDTH AND LENGTH.

The Amazon rainforest in South America is the world's largest tropical rainforest. It covers an area of 5.5 million square kilometres. The rainforest takes its name from the Amazon river, a network of waterways that stretch for 6,840 kilometres (km).

Different tribes living in the Amazon rainforest each have their own language and culture. Some have never had contact with the outside world.

AMAZON TRIBES

Groups of indigenous people, called tribes, have lived in the Amazon rainforest for thousands of years. There are some tribes that rely on the rainforest for all their needs, including food, medicine and clothes.

The Amazon rainforest is home to thousands of animal species, including one of the world's largest spiders – the Goliath birdeater. It feeds on mice, earthworms, frogs and birds. This spider injects poison into its victim using its long fangs.

GOLIATH BIRDEATER

Capybaras live in groups along riverbanks. Capybara young are sometimes eaten by caimans that hide in the river. Other animals that live in the river include manatees, red-bellied piranha fish, which have razor-sharp teeth, and dolphins.

CAPYBARAS

The black caiman can reach up to five metres in length, over three times longer than an average human's height.

BLACK CAIMAN

23

THREATS TO
RAINFORESTS

Rainforests are under threat due to deforestation – the cutting down and removal of trees from a forested area. More than half the world's rainforests have already been destroyed to provide timber and space for farming, mining and building.

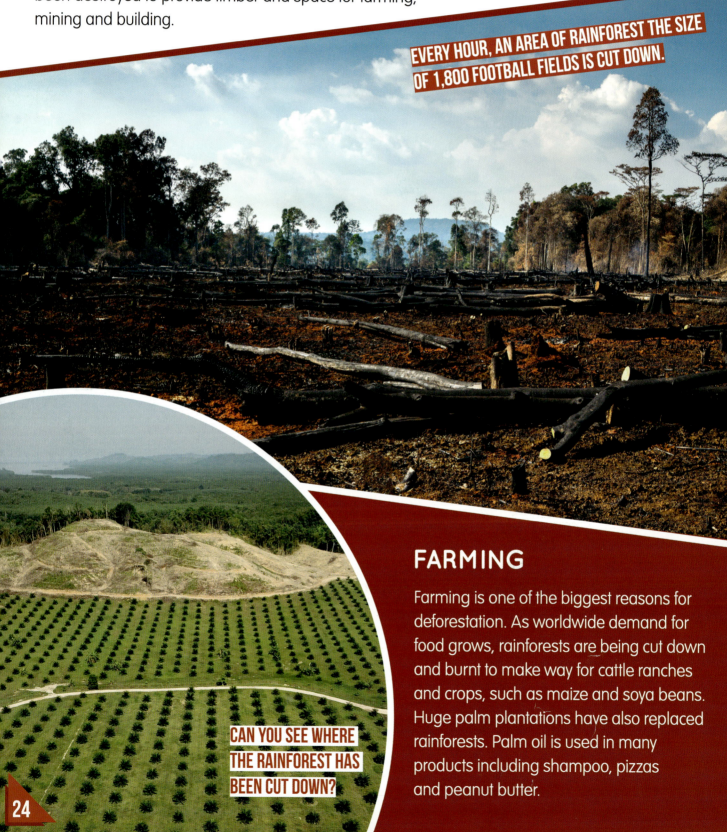

EVERY HOUR, AN AREA OF RAINFOREST THE SIZE OF 1,800 FOOTBALL FIELDS IS CUT DOWN.

CAN YOU SEE WHERE THE RAINFOREST HAS BEEN CUT DOWN?

FARMING

Farming is one of the biggest reasons for deforestation. As worldwide demand for food grows, rainforests are being cut down and burnt to make way for cattle ranches and crops, such as maize and soya beans. Huge palm plantations have also replaced rainforests. Palm oil is used in many products including shampoo, pizzas and peanut butter.

MINING

Large areas of rainforest have been removed, especially in the Amazon basin, to allow mining of metals, such as copper, iron, gold and tin. Miners and loggers clear even more land to build roads to move their materials around. Mining also causes pollution and soil damage that makes it hard for trees to regrow.

HYDROELECTRIC POWER STATION

HYDROELECTRIC ENERGY

Hydroelectric energy plants use water to make electricity. Large dams and **reservoirs** are needed to hold the water used to produce the electricity. Huge areas of rainforest, especially in Brazil, have been flooded to make way for them.

RAINFORESTS AND GLOBAL WARMING

Global warming is the slow rise in temperatures on Earth. It is caused by greenhouse gases. These are gases on Earth that trap heat from the Sun and stop it from being reflected back into space. Carbon dioxide is a greenhouse gas. Burning rainforests, like the burning of **fossil fuels** such as coal and oil, produces large amounts of carbon dioxide. It is thought to be an important cause of global warming. Global warming is leading to the melting of the polar ice caps, rising sea levels, floods, droughts and wildfires.

♥ earth

there is no planet B

SOME PEOPLE TAKE PART IN DEMONSTRATIONS TO RAISE AWARENESS OF GLOBAL WARMING.

Many animals are losing habitats because of global warming, including polar bears, which live on the Arctic sea ice.

Rainforests remove carbon dioxide from the Earth's atmosphere and caring for them is one of the best ways of tackling global warming. Rainforests are sometimes referred to as the 'lungs of the planet'. Rainforests also play an important part in maintaining the Earth's supply of fresh water. Rainforest plants release **water vapour** from their leaves, which forms clouds and eventually falls as rain.

Fresh water is very important. It provides people with clean drinking water. Deforestation affects how much fresh water we have.

RAINFOREST RECOVERY

We can all help the rainforests to recover. Make sure that any rainforest products your family buys, such as bananas, carry a Rainforest Alliance Certified sticker.

Rainforest Alliance stickers have a green frog on them. These products have been made or grown while looking after the rainforest.

Look at the ingredients lists on products. Try to avoid buying items containing palm oil.

PALM OIL COMES FROM THE FLESH OF THE OIL PALM FRUIT AND FROM THE SEED INSIDE.

If your family buys anything made of wood, check to see if it is wood from a rainforest tree. If it is, you could suggest something made from a different type of wood.

ECOTOURISM

Ecotourism is a form of travel that supports natural environments, such as rainforests. Local people can earn money by guiding tourists and providing places to stay and eat, rather than by cutting down the rainforests for farming.

CHARITIES

Many charities are trying to protect rainforests and the threatened plant and animal species in them. They aim to stop deforestation and to plant as many new trees as possible. They also work with local people to find ways of farming that give farmers a fair wage, and that look after natural resources.

Ecotourism brings money to local people and allows tourists to enjoy the rainforests without damaging them.

Planting trees helps to repair the damage done by deforestation.

YOUR FAMILY COULD JOIN A CHARITY SUCH AS THE WWF (WORLD WILDLIFE FUND). YOU CAN FIND OUT MORE ON THEIR WEBSITE: WWW.WORLDWILDLIFE.ORG

FASCINATING FACTS

Some of the longest rivers in the world flow through tropical rainforests. As well as the Amazon, they include the Congo (4,700 km), the Mekong (4,350 km) and the Orinoco (2,140 km).

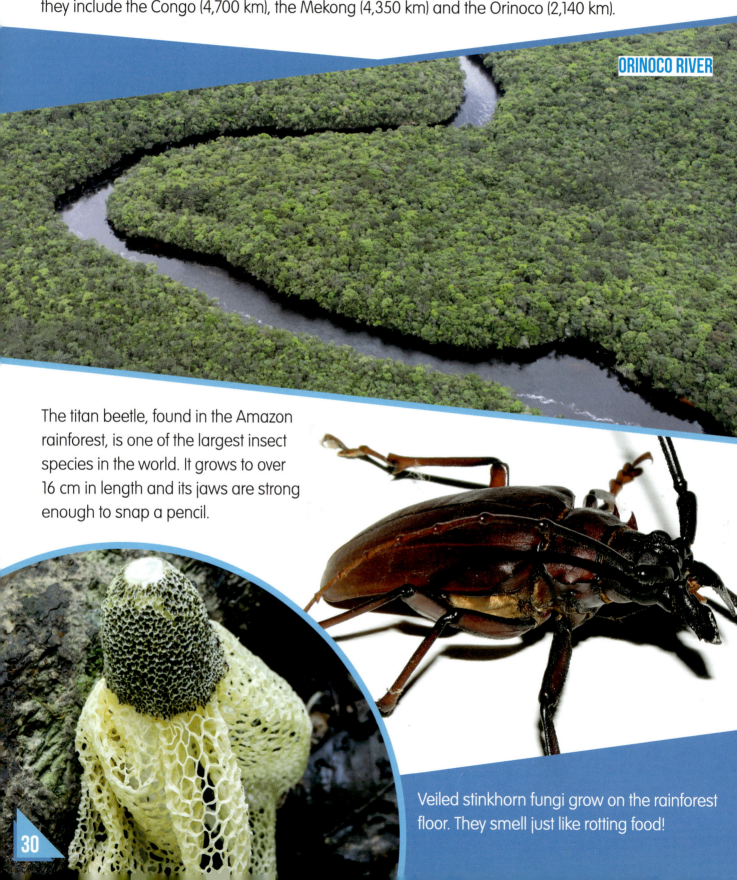

ORINOCO RIVER

The titan beetle, found in the Amazon rainforest, is one of the largest insect species in the world. It grows to over 16 cm in length and its jaws are strong enough to snap a pencil.

Veiled stinkhorn fungi grow on the rainforest floor. They smell just like rotting food!

GLOSSARY

adapted   changed over time to suit the environment

algae   a plant or plant-like living thing that has no roots, stems, leaves or flowers

camouflaged   using colours and patterns to blend in and hide in a habitat

carbon dioxide   a colourless gas found in the atmosphere and in the air that humans breathe out

cosmetics   treatments and medicines used to make someone look better

food chain   a series of living things that all rely on the next as a source of food

fossil fuels   sources of energy, such as coal, oil and gas, that formed millions of years ago from the remains of animals and plants

fungi   simple living organisms that are neither plants nor animals

habitats   the natural homes in which animals, plants and other living things live

humid   air containing a high level of water; damp

mammals   animals that have warm blood, a backbone and produce milk for their young

microorganisms   tiny organisms, such as bacteria, that are too small to be seen with the naked eye

mosses   a type of plant that has no roots or flowers, and covers things like a carpet

nutrients   natural substances that plants and animals need in order to grow and stay healthy

predators   animals that hunt other animals for food

prey   animals that are hunted by other animals for food

reptiles   cold-blooded, scaly animals that have a backbone

reservoirs   huge lakes or ponds created by dams

species   a group of very similar animals or plants that can create young together

water vapour   water that is in the form of gas and below boiling temperature

INDEX

CUMBRIA LIBRARIES

3 8003 05176 0627

This book is on loan from
Library Services for Schools
**www.cumbria.gov.uk/
libraries/schoolslibserv**

County Council